SHOCK ZONE

VILLAINS

W9-ACR-319

MERCILESS Monarchs AND RUTHLESS ROYALTY

MIRIAM ARONIN

Lerner Publications Company • Minneapolis

With love and gratitude to my family and friends, who are fortunately neither royal nor villians.

—MA

Lerner Publications Company
A division of Lerner Publishing Group, Inc.
241 First Avenue North
Minneapolis, MN 55401 U.S.A.

Website address: www.lernerbooks.com

Library of Congress Cataloging-in-Publication Data

Aronin, Miriam.
    Merciless monarchs and ruthless royalty / by Miriam Aronin.
        p.   cm. — (ShockZone™—Villains)
    Includes index.
    ISBN 978–1–4677–0607–0 (lib. bdg. : alk. paper)
        1. Kings and rulers—Biography—Juvenile literature. I. Title.
    D107.A74 2013
    321.0092'2—dc23   2012027291

Manufactured in the United States of America
1 – CG – 12/31/12

TABLE OF CONTENTS

ROYAL VILLAINS

What do you think of when you hear the word *royal*? **Fairy-tale kings and queens?** Handsome princes and beautiful princesses? Golden crowns and gleaming palaces? Well, check your history books. Real-life royals weren't always so squeaky-clean. In fact, some were closer to storybook villains. Many were downright mean and nasty.

England's Queen Victoria and Prince Albert, who ruled in the 1800s, weren't ruthless. But some of their ancestors certainly were.

Some kings or queens would stop at nothing to gain power. These merciless monarchs murdered anyone who got in their way. No one was safe—not even their own brothers, sons, mothers, and wives. Some were greedy for land, loot, or riches. They usually got what they wanted. They didn't care how. Blackmail? Bloody battles? Raids and robbery? These ruthless rulers were up for anything.

monarchs = kings or queens who rule over a kingdom or an empire

Some had hot tempers and a taste for revenge. Some made harsh laws and ordered fearsome punishments. Their enemies—and often their own subjects—lived in terror of torture and death. After learning about these brutal royals from the past, you'll be glad none of them are your leaders!

King Herod the Not-So-Great
(r. 37-4 B.C.)

King Herod is often called Herod the Great. But the way he treated his family? Not great. Not great at all.

Herod became king of Judea (a region of the Middle East) in 37 B.C. when the Roman army helped him overthrow the previous ruler. The new king was eager to show off his greatness. He built the port city of Caesarea on the Mediterranean Sea. He built a grand palace inside a fortress he named Herodium. He rebuilt the Jewish Temple in Jerusalem with great splendor.

Herod's massive building projects made him famous. But he was always on the lookout for threats to his power. Anyone he saw as a threat had to die. Many of his victims were part of his own family.

Before Herod, Judea was ruled by the Hasmonean family. Many Judeans still supported their old rulers instead of King Herod. Fearing the old rulers' power, Herod decided to marry into the family. He took the beautiful Hasmonean princess Mariamne for his wife.

That wasn't enough for Herod, though. To protect his crown, he had his new wife's grandfather and brother Joseph brutally murdered. Years later, he suspected that Mariamne had been unfaithful. So he killed her too. Was he sorry? Maybe. Legend tells that he kept his beloved Mariamne's body preserved in honey for seven years. Herod was not sorry enough to stop butchering his family, though. He later had his own two sons executed.

At the end of his life, Herod became very sick. He suffered terrible pain in both his mind and body. Think that would've softened him? Not exactly. After a group of Jews tried to remove a Roman symbol from the Temple gate, he had forty-two people burned. At last, this cruel ruler died in agony in 4 B.C.

Part of the Temple built under Herod still stands in modern Jerusalem. It makes up the lower part of the Western Wall.

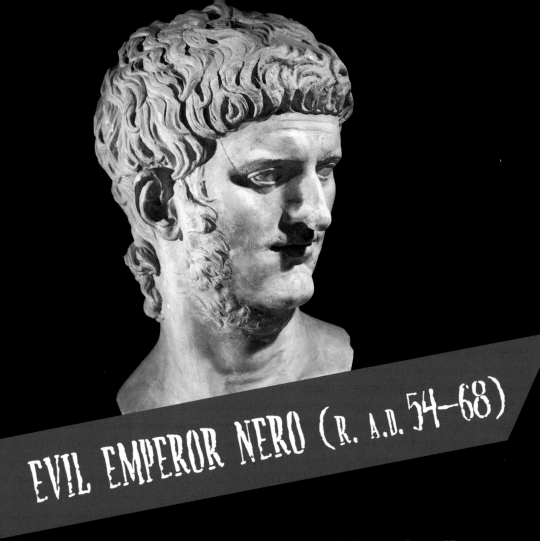

EVIL EMPEROR NERO (R. A.D. 54–68)

The Roman Emperor Nero came from a ruthless family. The emperors before him had plundered Rome's treasury and murdered anyone who stood in their way. And then there was Nero's mother, Agrippina. She would do anything to put her son on the throne. First, she married the Emperor Claudius. Then she got him out of the way—with poison.

plundered = took or used up wrongfully

In A.D. 54, Nero became the new emperor. But Agrippina hadn't cared about helping her son. She just wanted to rule through him. Nero had other ideas. In 59 he had Agrippina killed. Three years later, he feared his wife Octavia was turning people against him after he fell for another woman. So he killed Octavia too.

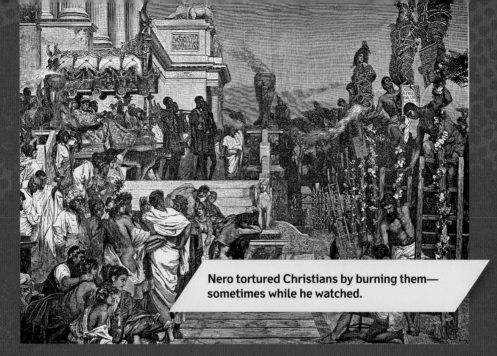

Nero tortured Christians by burning them—sometimes while he watched.

In 64 a huge fire raged in Rome for almost a week. Much of the city was destroyed. Nero knew people blamed him for the fire. So he found someone else to blame. Christians were a small religious group at the time. They were an easy target. Many Romans already thought they practiced wicked acts. Nero had Christians arrested. Then he tortured them to death in public.

Nero spent a fortune on fancy new buildings and often acted wildly in public. The Romans became fed up with their emperor. In 68 they revolted. Nero had to flee the city. The government declared him a public enemy. But Nero spared them the trouble of hunting him down. That same year, the evil emperor killed himself.

FIDDLING WHILE ROME BURNED?

Legend has it that Nero fiddled while Rome burned. That's not *exactly* true. There were no fiddles (violins) in Nero's time. But he did like to write poetry, sing, and play the lyre—a small, guitarlike instrument. So he could've been doing something just as inappropriate during his city's tragedy.

Nero wanted to project himself as a god-like emperor, so he had his own image engraved on Roman coins.

Vlad the Impaler (r. 1456–1476):
REAL-LIFE DRACULA

Vlad III Dracula wasn't a vampire. But he was just as bloodthirsty. Vlad's story starts in 1448 when his father was assassinated by his boyars. Young Vlad tried to take his father's place as prince of Walachia, part of modern-day Romania. But Hungarian and Ottoman Turkish forces were battling for control of the area. They kept Vlad off the throne.

> **boyars =**
> members of an eastern European or Russian noble class

After eight long years of fighting, Vlad claimed his crown in 1456. His fight wasn't over, though. He wanted to kick the Ottomans out of Walachia for good. And he wanted revenge. After each battle, Vlad had defeated enemy soldiers impaled—he stuck sharp wooden stakes through their bodies. Then he left them to die in agony.

> **stakes =**
> pointed wooden sticks

A NEW DRACULA

In 1897 Bram Stoker wrote the spine-tingling novel *Dracula*, set near Walachia. Many people think Stoker's bloodthirsty vampire Count Dracula was based partly on Vlad the Impaler.

Vlad the Impaler was just as cruel to his own people. Stories tell that he would impale his subjects for any misdeed, no matter how tiny. You could face that awful death if you were caught stealing or telling a lie—or even not taking proper care of your clothing.

The heartless prince also had no use for anyone who could not work. According to one story, he invited all the poor and sick in Walachia to a great feast. At the end of the feast, he set the building on fire. Inside, all his guests were burned alive.

This wood carving depicts Vlad dining in front of his impaled victims.

In 1462 Hungarian forces took Vlad prisoner. He was freed and returned to the throne in 1476. Luckily, he did not rule for long this time. He was killed in battle that same year.

RICHARD III (R. 1483–1485):
A ROYAL MURDER MYSTERY

Did Richard III of England murder his way to the top? We may never know for sure. This wily king left behind no proof. But many historians believe that Richard was a killer.

Richard grew up with war. He was only three years old when the Wars of the Roses broke out in 1455. In these bloody wars, two noble families were fighting to rule England. One of them was Richard's. Henry VI led the other.

Before Richard's tenth birthday, his older brother became King Edward IV. Ten years later, Edward defeated Henry VI in battle. Edward ordered Henry put to death. They didn't leave a record of who carried out the order. But Richard is a top suspect.

In 1483 Edward died. He left behind two young sons. The older son, aged twelve, was next in line for the crown. But Richard was not the type to let a couple of kids keep him off the throne. He brought the young king and prince to London. He promised to help and protect them. You can guess how much that promise was worth. By the end of the year, the boys had disappeared. Rumors about their deaths were flying.

Richard became king—but not for long. The Wars of the Roses were still raging, and allies of the rival noble family wanted Richard out. Richard's final punishment came in 1485. He was killed at the Battle of Bosworth Field, the rivalry's last great clash.

Did Richard have his two nephews murdered in the Tower of London? That's what some people believe.

AHUIZOTL (r. 1486-1502):
AZTEC WARRIOR KING

Ahuizotl (ah-WEE-tzoh-tuhl) became king of the Aztec Empire, in Central America, in 1486. But he could not be crowned right away. As a new *tlatoani,* or king, he had to fight a war first. Ahuizotl won a great victory in his first war. His army came home loaded with riches and prisoners.

To celebrate, Ahuizotl was crowned in a grand ceremony. People came from far and wide to honor the powerful king. But some leaders in the area didn't show. The king was furious. There was only one answer to such an insult. He would go to war again—this time against the territories of those absent leaders.

The new war was a huge success. Ahuizotl took thousands of prisoners. The captives faced a bloody doom. Soon they would be offered as a sacrifice to the Aztec gods.

sacrifice =
something offered
to a god, usually
the life of a living
being

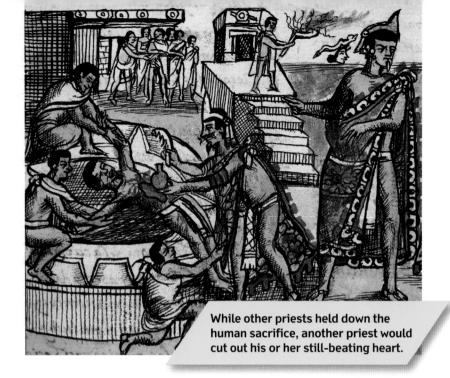

While other priests held down the human sacrifice, another priest would cut out his or her still-beating heart.

The Aztecs had just finished building a spectacular temple in their capital city of Tenochtitlán. The time had come to dedicate it—with human blood.

The sacrifices took place in the new temple. It stood atop a towering pyramid. To reach the top, prisoners climbed 114 steps. For four days, long lines of prisoners climbed up to the temple. At the top, Aztec priests cut the victims' bodies open with sharp knives. Then the priests tore out the victims' hearts.

WAR AND RICHES

War was a big part of Aztec life. Aztec raiders brought home loot that made their cities rich. Two of the most sought-after valuables were jade and cacao. Jade is a precious stone. It often has a green color. Jade can be carved into jewelry and all kinds of beautiful objects. Cacao seedpods grow on trees. Today, cacao is used to make chocolate.

Ahuizotl did not just watch the bloodbath. With his own hands, he helped tear out the victims' hearts. Blood flowed like a red river back down the pyramid steps. It gushed past the waiting prisoners. Reports claimed that Ahuizotl had up to twenty thousand people sacrificed at the temple. Later, the bodies were burned. The skulls were saved on long racks inside the temple.

Ahuizotl forced rival leaders to watch the parade of gruesome deaths. He wanted to make sure they would always fear the Aztecs. But after that terrifying spectacle, he just wanted to entertain. He showered guests with music and gifts that showed off his riches.

For more than a decade, Ahuizotl continued to live grandly. How did he pay for his palaces and banquets? He demanded tribute payments from other towns. If they did not pay, he went to war.

tribute = payment from one nation or leader to a higher ruler

You did not want to get on the fierce warrior's bad side. In fifteen years, he conquered forty-five towns. And he was big on revenge. Around 1497 several Aztec traders were killed in other villages. Ahuizotl ordered his fighters into the villages. He told them to kill two thousand villagers for each dead trader.

Around 1502 a great flood swept through Tenochtitlán. Historians think Ahuizotl died while trying to escape. Two hundred of his slaves were picked to go with him to the afterlife. Priests tore out the slaves' hearts. Then the bodies were burned. It was Ahuizotl's last sacrifice.

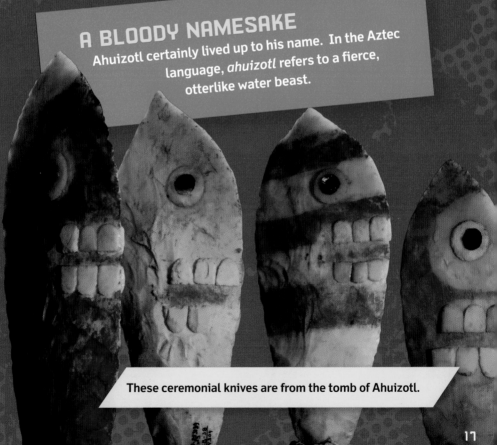

A BLOODY NAMESAKE

Ahuizotl certainly lived up to his name. In the Aztec language, *ahuizotl* refers to a fierce, otterlike water beast.

These ceremonial knives are from the tomb of Ahuizotl.

Ivan the Terrible (r. 1533–1584)

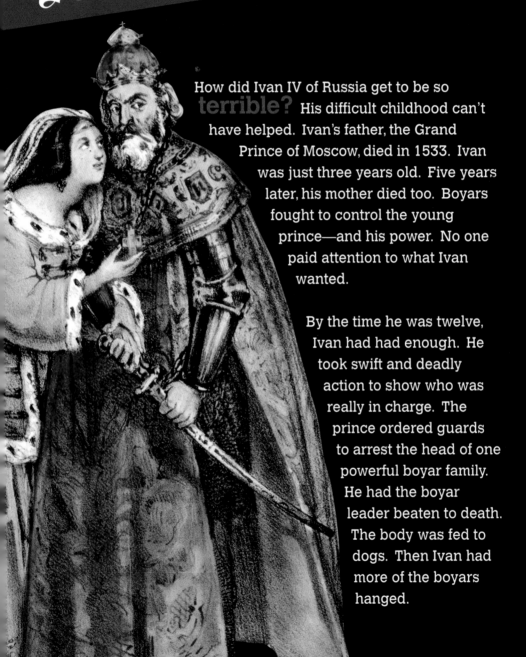

How did Ivan IV of Russia get to be so **terrible?** His difficult childhood can't have helped. Ivan's father, the Grand Prince of Moscow, died in 1533. Ivan was just three years old. Five years later, his mother died too. Boyars fought to control the young prince—and his power. No one paid attention to what Ivan wanted.

By the time he was twelve, Ivan had had enough. He took swift and deadly action to show who was really in charge. The prince ordered guards to arrest the head of one powerful boyar family. He had the boyar leader beaten to death. The body was fed to dogs. Then Ivan had more of the boyars hanged.

Ivan had Saint Basil's Cathedral built in Moscow, Russia, to honor his capture of Kazan and Astrakhan.

Soon Ivan was old enough to be officially crowned. But he didn't want to be just a prince of Moscow. Instead, in 1547 Ivan IV became the first czar of all Russia. The new title implied that Ivan had more power and a God-given right to the throne. The czar conquered the lands of Kazan and Astrakhan on the Volga River. Then he turned north and west to Livonia, in modern-day Latvia and Estonia. This new war went badly. Around the same time, Ivan's beloved wife, Anastasia, died.

czar = or tsar; king or emperor of Russia

Furious, Ivan took out his anger on some of his closest advisers. He accused them of killing Anastasia. Soon they were dead. Ivan did not stop there. He had many of the men's family members and friends killed too.

WHY A CZAR?

The word *czar* comes from the word "Caesar," the title of the Roman emperor. Ivan wanted to rule a mighty empire, just like the Roman Empire. So he took the title "czar" to connect himself to the Roman leaders.

The oprichniki terrorized many people.

The nobles weren't the only ones who felt Ivan's wrath. After his wife died, Ivan created a crew of guards called *oprichniki*. Their main job was to steal families' homes and lands for Ivan. As long as the oprichniki did their job, they were free to kill or torture anyone they pleased. People lived in fear of the czar's brutal men.

In early 1570, Ivan turned his attention to the well-off Russian city of Novgorod. He said the city's leaders were loyal to his enemy, the king of Poland. As punishment, Ivan's guards raided the city. They stole all the food and clothing they could find. They burned some citizens to death. Others were thrown into an icy river to drown. In just six weeks, thousands of people died.

Ivan may have been sorry for his cruelty in the end. In 1581 the czar got into a fight with his oldest son. The czar hit twenty-seven-year-old Prince Ivan in the head with a heavy stick. The younger Ivan was badly wounded. He died five days later.

killing. He had lost his son and heir. He decided to make a list of the people he had killed so they would be remembered. Ivan the Terrible died in 1584. By then his list included more than three thousand names.

heir = a person who inherits property, such as a kingdom or empire

FROM PEASANTS TO SERFS

Ivan's wars were expensive. To pay for them, he charged landowners high taxes. The landowners tried to pass along the costs to the peasants who farmed their land. Many peasants could not pay. So they left their land instead. To stop them, Ivan made it illegal for the farmworkers to move. They became serfs, bound by law to work the same land.

BLOODY MARY
(R. 1553–1558)

Women rulers can be just as bloody as men. Take Mary I of England. When Mary came to the throne in 1553, deadly conflicts over religion were breaking out all over Europe. Protestants were starting to challenge the Roman Catholic Church.

Protestants = certain groups of Christians that do not follow the Roman Catholic Church

Mary was a firm Catholic. But when she became queen, England was not a Catholic country. Her father, Henry VIII, had split from the Catholic Church in order to end his marriage with Mary's mother. It's no surprise that their daughter was not a fan of the new Protestant Church of England.

When Henry died, his son Edward VI became king. Then, six years later, Edward died. Mary was next in line for the crown. At last, she could return the country to her Catholic faith.

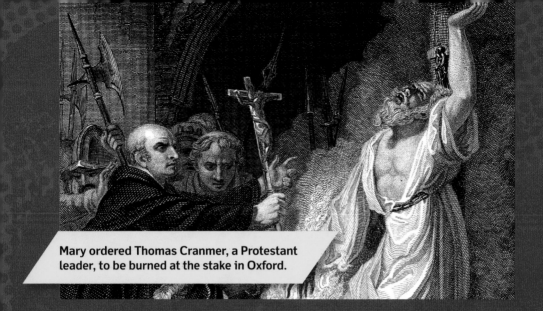

Mary ordered Thomas Cranmer, a Protestant leader, to be burned at the stake in Oxford.

Mary started by outlawing the Church of England. Then, in 1554, she made all heresy against the Catholic Church a crime. People found guilty of holding to Protestant beliefs faced a painful fate. They were burned at the stake—bound to a wooden stake and set atop a fire. If the wood was dry or the fire was large, they died quickly. Newly cut wood or a small fire burned more slowly. That made the torture even worse. One victim took forty-five minutes to die. In agony, he cried out for more fire so he would die faster.

heresy = believing ideas that are different from the teachings of a church or other religious group

Mary had around three hundred Protestants burned to death. She might have burned even more if she had lived longer. Mary died of an unknown illness in 1558.

Queen Mary arrived in London with her sister—before she had Princess Elizabeth imprisoned in the Tower.

After Mary's death, her half sister Elizabeth became queen. Elizabeth I returned England to their father's church. England's official church has been Protestant ever since.

CIXI (r. 1861–1908):
POWER-HUNGRY EMPRESS

China's Dowager Empress Cixi (Tsoo-Shee) never ruled on her own. But she was always on **the lookout for power.**

dowager = title of a noble or wealthy widow

Cixi was just one of the Chinese Emperor Xianfeng's many wives. But she had a special role. She was the mother of his first son. In 1861, when the child was five, the emperor died. The young boy took the throne.

Cixi's forces ended the rebellion when they attacked Nanjing in 1864.

Cixi became one of his regents. That meant she would help run the government until her son was old enough to rule on his own.

As regent, Cixi showed no mercy to her enemies. Another regent named Su Shun had schemed to take over. The empress declared him a traitor. He was beheaded in the public market. And she showed no mercy to rebels, who wanted a new system of government. The Taiping Rebellion had been building its army for years. Cixi sent generals to crush it by any means necessary. In 1864 in the city of Nanjing, one hundred thousand rebels were killed.

In 1873 Cixi's son turned seventeen, old enough to rule on his own. Cixi stepped down as regent. But the young emperor died just two years later. One of his wives was pregnant at the time. If she had a boy, the child would be emperor. And the boy's mother—not Cixi—would become regent.

Cixi's son, Tongzhi, didn't rule for long.

This printed artwork shows Cixi inspecting the heads of those who betrayed her.

However, the emperor's pregnant wife died before the baby was born. Rumors flew. Had the emperor been poisoned? Had his wife been murdered? Was Cixi responsible? Probably not. But with no one in her way, it seems that she had every intention of regaining power.

The empress suspected that some palace guards might not be loyal to her. She had them arrested and sent to prison. Then Cixi announced that she was adopting her nephew. That made him next in line to become emperor. The boy was just four years old. So Cixi—you guessed it—became ruler again as his regent.

In 1889 Cixi retired. She let her nephew take power as emperor. He tried to make reforms. He wanted China to have a more modern government. But many people were against his changes. In 1898 army officers forced him to give up power. They named Cixi regent one last time.

Things did not go well this time around. The country faced hunger and floods. Even worse, Europeans were invading China. The ruling family fled before the invaders arrived. Cixi's forces were too weak to drive them away. In the end, the Europeans forced the Chinese to sign a treaty giving up many rights. Many people blamed the empress.

Cixi died in 1908, shortly after she named a new emperor to the throne. He would be the last emperor of China. He ruled only until 1912.

The Forbidden City was once home to many emperors. Since 1925 it has housed the Palace Museum.

A ROYAL GRAVE
When Cixi died, her burial was fit for an empress. Her grave was full of pearls, diamonds, and other jewels. But she did not rest in peace. Twenty years later, Chinese soldiers returned to her grave. They stole all the jewels they could find.

LEOPOLD II (R. 1865-1909): A GLOBAL TYRANT

Leopold II became king of Belgium in 1865. But was that enough for him? No! In 1885 his forces invaded central Africa. He named the land they seized the Congo Free State. It was eighty times bigger than Belgium. It had many natural resources.

Leopold was the sovereign of the land. That meant he had unlimited power. He claimed he would work against the slave trade, which forced the Congo's peoples into slavery. He promised to make living conditions better.

sovereign = supreme ruler

Really, though, the greedy king could not wait to get his hands on the Congo's riches, especially its rubber trees. The trees produce a liquid that can be tapped and made into rubber products. Demand for these products was booming. The king stood to make a fortune.

Rubber drips out of a tree for a few hours when a sliver of bark is removed.

Leopold never visited the Congo. His agents and soldiers did the dirty work for him. They forced Congolese men to harvest liquid rubber from trees. The men were treated like slaves. They were never paid. They lived in terror. If they did not bring back as much rubber as the agents demanded, the punishments were brutal. Soldiers might hack off a man's hand. They might kill his wife and children. Or they might burn down his whole village.

About 10 million Congolese people died as a result of Leopold's greedy demands. Missionaries and others working in the Congo were horrified at the violence. They wrote letters and published shocking articles about the bloodbath. People around the world took notice. At last, in 1908, the Belgian government took over control of the Congo. The king died the next year.

missionaries = people who work to spread the Christian religion

The Congo became an independent country in 1960. Sadly, it still struggles with violence and poor living conditions—long-lasting effects of Leopold's cruelty.

These children lost their hands during the reign of Leopold.

Buchanan, Jane. *Mary Tudor: Courageous Queen or Bloody Mary?* New York: Franklin Watts, 2008.
Want to read more about the life and times of Bloody Mary? Then this book is right up your alley.

Donovan, Sandy. *Lethal Leaders and Military Madmen.* Minneapolis: Lerner Publications Company, 2013.
Not all ruthless rulers are royalty! These cruel villains weren't born to the throne, but they were just as bloodthirsty as the merciless monarchs you just read about.

Mary I (r. 1553–1558)
http://www.royal.gov.uk/historyofthemonarchy/kingsandqueensofengland/thetudors/maryi.aspx
Check out the official website of the British monarchy to find more information on how Bloody Mary went after heretics.

Price, Sean. *Ivan the Terrible: Tsar of Death.* New York: Franklin Watts, 2008.
Want more information on what made Ivan so terrible? You can find lots of gory details in this biography of Russia's tyrannical first czar.

Price, Sean Stewart. *Cixi: Evil Empress of China?* New York: Franklin Watts, 2008.
Venture inside the Forbidden Palace in this detailed biography and get the real story of China's last empress.

Richard III (r. 1483–1485)
http://www.royal.gov.uk/HistoryoftheMonarchy/KingsandQueensofEngland/TheYorkists/RichardIII.aspx
Intrigued by the historical mysteries of Richard III? Check out the fact-filled official website of the British monarchy.

Streissguth, Tom. *Queen Cleopatra.* Minneapolis: Lerner Publications Company, 2007.
Read all about yet another notorious royal. Was she one more royal villain? Read the book and then decide.

INDEX

The images in this book are used with the permission of: © After Franz Xavier Winterhalter/The Bridgeman Art Library/Getty Images, p. 4; © Guildhall Art Gallery, City of London/The Bridgeman Art Library, p. 5; © Germanisches National Museum, Nuremberg (Nuernberg), Germany/The Bridgeman Art Library, p. 6; © John & Lisa Merill/The Image Bank/Getty Images, p. 7; © De Agostini Picture Library/Getty Images, p. 8; © Kean Collection/Archive Photos/Getty Images, p. 9 (top); © Hoberman Collection/UIG via Getty Images, p. 9 (bottom); © Stock Montage/Archive Photos/ Getty Images, p. 10; Universal/Kobal Collection/Art Resource, NY, p. 11 (top); © Marsden Archive/SuperStock, p. 11 (bottom); © Society of Antiquaries of London, UK/The Bridgeman Art Library, p. 12; © Robbie Jack/CORBIS, p. 13 (top); The Granger Collection, New York, p. 13 (bottom); © American Illustrators Gallery, NYC/www. asapworldwide.com/The Bridgeman Art Library, p. 14; © G. Dagli Orti/De Agostini Picture Library/Getty Images, p. 15 (top); © Lawrence Lim/Dorling Kindersley/Getty Images, p. 15 (bottom); © DeAgostini/SuperStock, p. 16; © Kenneth Grant/National Geographic Image Collection/Alamy, p. 17; Rue des Archives/The Granger Collection, New York, p. 18; © Walter Bibikow/The Image Bank/Getty Images, p. 19 (top); © Kremlin Museums, Moscow, Russia/Hirmer Fotoarchiv/The Bridgeman Art Library, p. 19 (bottom); © Look and Learn/The Bridgeman Art Library, p. 20; © Image Asset Management Ltd./SuperStock, p. 21; © Hulton Archive/Hulton Royals Collection/Getty Images, pp. 22, 27 (inset), 28; © Universal History Archive/Universal Images Group/ Getty Images, pp. 23 (top), 24; © Palace of Westminster, London, UK/The Bridgeman Art Library, p. 23 (bottom); © Eileen Tweedy/The Art Archive at Art Resource, NY, p. 25 (top); © Hu Weibiao/Panorama/The Image Works, p. 25 (bottom); © Visual Arts Publishing Limited/The Bridgeman Art Library, p. 26; © Tom Bonaventure/Digital Vision/Getty Images, p. 27 (background); © Richard Choy/Peter Arnold/Getty Images, p. 29 (top); © Universal Images Group/SuperStock, p. 29 (bottom).

Front cover: © The Bridgeman Art Library/Getty Images.

Main body text set in Calvert MT Std Regular 11/16.
Typeface provided by Monotype Typography.